THE RECEIVER

OTHER BOOKS BY SHARON THESEN

Artemis Hates Romance (1980)
Radio New France Radio (1981)
Holding the Pose (1983)
Confabulations (1984)
The Beginning of the Long Dash (1987)
The Pangs of Sunday: Selected Poems (1990)
Aurora (1995)
News and Smoke: Selected Poems (1999)
A Pair of Scissors (2000)
Weeping Willow (2005)
The Good Bacteria (2006)
Oyama Pink Shale (2011)

The Receiver

SHARON THESEN

VANCOUVER ▼ NEW STAR BOOKS ▼ 2017

NEW STAR BOOKS LTD.
107 – 3477 Commercial Street, Vancouver, BC V5N 4E8   CANADA
1574 Gulf Road, No. 1517, Point Roberts, WA 98281   USA
www.NewStarBooks.com   info@NewStarBooks.com

Copyright Sharon Thesen 2017. All rights reserved. No part of this work may be reproduced, stored in a retrieval system or transmitted, in any form or by any means, without the prior written consent of the publisher or a licence from Access Copyright.

The publisher acknowledges the financial support of the Canada Council for the Arts and the British Columbia Arts Council.

Cataloguing information for this book is available from Library and Archives Canada, www.collectionscanada.gc.ca.

Cover design by Robin Mitchell Cranfield
Cover photo by CatalpaSpirit
Printed on 100% post-consumer recycled paper
Printed and bound in Canada by Gauvin Press
First published September 2017

and all the back country, the roads I have ridden
without headlights the moon was so bright on the houses

                                                CHARLES OLSON

there is no sacrosanct version,
there is only time

                                                C.D. WRIGHT

Contents

THE RECEIVER

The Receiver   3
Morning Walk by the Lake   6
The Gold Cure   8
The Old Church   10
The Magic of Paths   11
Quiet Mountain   12
I Was the Fifth Car Back   14
The Car Wash   16
Peak Oil   17
Anonymous   20
I Thought of Shelley   22
The War Against the Imagination   24

MY EDUCATION AS A POET

Vernon, 1954   31
At My Mother's in Prince George   32
Talking to My Mother on the Phone   36
Auntie Eileen   38
Uncle Dave   42
Pleasant St.   44
Churchgoing   47
Another Poem for My Mother   49
The Oddness of Elegy   51
My Education as a Poet   53

AROUND THEN

Anna Akhmatova   61
Four Books Side by Side on the Shelf   63
The Pangs of Sunday   67
Daphne In the Headphones   68
Churchgoing (2)   71
A Tourist Church in Drome-Provence   72

    CHARLES, FRANCES, RALPH AND ME   73

    BOOK OF MOTZ   75

THE RECEIVER

The Receiver

In a dream the other night
I was on the phone, one of those rotary-dial
black desk phones & looking out the window — a
window you lift up from the bottom
to stick your head outside to a night-time scene
as in Jean Cocteau's *The Human Voice*

— Ingrid Bergman's lover in a phone booth out on the street
where cars pass in the rain. It takes him a while to dial.
Coins pushed into the slot.

The Human Voice is a one-woman show,
all her side of the conversation
but I don't remember anything she actually says.

There is a lot of murmuring, perhaps some pleading, some
push-back. She's lying on the bed crying, they'd hang up,
then the phone would ring once more. She'd lean into
the receiver, her beautiful voice and mouth, and
breaking heart. I imagine the receiver holding
the whole story inside.

In my heart a dream once presided of respite
and within that dream the small silver key to unlock it.
Respite from worries, from pleading with fate.
But, as Camus insists,
Sisyphus was happy, bound only to his fate & nothing else.

I imagine Sisyphus glancing outward
at the top of his effort to check which constellation
shone upon him then, whose story
fixed its fixed eye upon him

— condemned for what? I wonder.
I should google the myth of Sisyphus
and while I'm at it,
the myth of this
and the myth of that.

*

People lying on the beach will tend to murmur
but seldom converse. Albert Camus says the sun is God,
that we have exiled beauty, and that the body
is happiest in sunshine, in a sea-blue and sun-yellow world.

Other worlds have their charms and attractions,
more nuanced and even more hopeful
than the straw hats of others just off the plane
from Cabo San Lucas or Honolulu.

How would we know they were happy?
we might ask.
A tan.

*

It was one of those rotary-dial phones that sat on a credenza —
the kind you always answered.
These phones rang in Hollywood movies for many many
     years.
A dame in an evening gown would stride over,
pick up the receiver, say hello, and glare at the fellow

holding her ermine stole. It will be awhile before everything
is sorted out, and this is why it's a story.

There would be whirlwinds of emotion such as someone
    might feel
returning from the plunge pools of Puerto Vallarta to the
    chilly rays of March
and testamental trees' fretful, cursive branches
in which an owl might sit saying hoo-hoo-hoo
& you would say who, me? And it would say yes, you.

You might wind up playing a role you only dreamed of
such as being a human voice in a telephone receiver,
the kind you had to lift out of what was called the cradle
and replace afterwards in the cradle's prongs. When it rang
    again
with a sharp European ring she knew it would be him, she
    knew
it would be eternal, so she lifted the receiver once more.

Morning Walk by the Lake

Pebbles and feathers,
bars of goose poop & geese smiling
and paddling not far from shore, glinting and satisfied,
large and a nuisance like my too-big dog

and I trotting by somebody's front window
pretty much on the dot of 9
on the newly revealed path strewn with
pressed-down pine needles since the snow left

orange and gold over the black damp earth,
stiff greenery to one side, saskatoon branches on the other,
just us, the geese, the ducks, a whistle from above —

a hawk? they have that sweet whistle
as they float by up in the wind currents
yellow-eyed & full of grace —

remnants of bleached lawn chairs still converse,
logs pulled up and arranged, signs posted for the poison ivy,
bulging roots spray-painted red, for safety,

a *losing battle* jokes someone whose dog
has a face exactly halved black and white,

the lake grey and glossy, fossil water from eons ago
nudging to shore in small waves, and deeper
than we knew, in fact deepest not far from here —

not that she lets on, particularly.

The Gold Cure

Limpid, decadent warmth in Davos
in the summertime, where consumptives once
lightly fried on the verandahs of the Berghof Schatzalp

"the magic mountain" of Thomas Mann's imagination & lived
in dreams and numerologies, where time
was not time but a thing

and to be there was to be a character
in an opera or a ballet in which a patient might
take the role of the faun in *Afternoon of a Faun*

a patient who'd only come to visit someone,
he forgets who, now, but here he is himself instead
such is the swiftness & efficiency of contagion

in this trapped condition on the mountaintop
where patients must fall in love eventually
with each other or the doctor

as we do in prisons, warehouses, spaceships,
schools, convents, labs, offices, outposts, boats,
due to proximity and a quasi-domestic dailiness

& which must be forbidden or managed
or not managed at all
through the boredom of the rest cure

or the throes of the toxic side-effects of the gold cure
because gold's atoms are tightly linked
and it is difficult to force them past each other.

The Old Church

The old church is more beautiful
than ever in its oldness and churchness   how was it
we never before noticed it, be it
ever so humble and out in the country

The parted trees of the entrance
latticed branches above
roots and bodies below the feathered beings
who appear in a space, like that hummingbird just did,
then flit zoom depart leaving you pregnant
with meaning

Who was it said "I wanted to say something"?
It took me a while to remember "Danse Russe"
by William Carlos Williams,
the one where the baby is sleeping and he dances
alone in his room, a poet

How is it you can regret
your own mind, & what you do, how you do it, and know
where your blind spots are & where you tend to go
and yet have to suffer in this being not another,
in your knowing, not another's.

The Magic of Paths

Any path is a path of least resistance.
It succumbs to the pull of gravity, avoids
the harshest rise. It rises up to meet you.
It flows around trees and lower bushes,
avoiding their tips and growth reach.

The walker treads lightly over boggy places,
presses more firmly when the downward slope
is steep. The legs and body follow the mind
& eyes, looking forward. Any path could be
an animal path, for the same
reason, the way a rise takes itself up
with itself, a rocky place eludes
your footing, a wet place avoids your
dry shoes. Ever ahead, a motion
leading by curves to the next limit.

In shadows paths disappear at the
crest of a hill then reappear
more deeply trodden, muddier & less inclined
as they spill and lighten.

On the flat, the wildflowers live despite
the onrush of walkers. Mothers with babies
trapped into contraptions, and an old good dog
or two, slow and talking. Societies
of path worlds.

Quiet Mountain

Spring not yet in full array.
Muddy and chilly. Flames were quiet
in the window of the stove
like goldfish smearing across aquarium glass.
Stove-light slurping up the walls.

It was all very fine. It was really quiet
of course being out in the country
with nobody nearby. It was paradise.

Mountains threw themselves out of lakes,
and, exemplars of peace and stillness,
looked-down-upon-us

yet cold, cold and steely grey
& patchy white, and this particular one,
the Quiet Mountain

cut into the sky and gave it shape,
held sweet fresh water in its fissures,
felt the cut of roads being built,
the wounding dynamite — and its neighbour,
a good friend they'd play mental chess
& telepathize reports of rivulets,
blueberries, porcupines

while we below were mute
and closed into our own thoughts.

I Was the Fifth Car Back

> (*found*, THE DAILY COURIER, *Jan. 21, 2011*)

I cannot for the life of me see
why this has been this way so long. Why
do only certain traffic lights have the left-turn signals
on the busiest, most-used road in Kelowna?
The traffic lights on those crossings with the directional lights
are not long enough. Timing them, I find
the majority are four to six seconds with three to four seconds
on amber. In this short window, four cars at most can turn
left and two can turn on the amber. The number that turn on
  red
only proves the green light is not long enough for the amount
of traffic wanting to turn.

Is it that difficult to see?
How many times have I sat in my car at Spall and Harvey,
no directional green arrow,
sixth car back,
and had to wait another three minutes to catch the next light?

How many times have I sat fuming
when the directional light turns green and the car
or two in front of me wastes two or three seconds
getting their butt in gear?

Sitting at Dilworth and Harvey recently,
waiting to turn left towards the lake,
there was no green arrow.
I was the fifth car back.
So much traffic was coming towards us from across the
　　highway,
the light turned red before the car in front of me could move.
So I sat waiting for the next green light.
The light was amber before it was clear
for me to turn, knowing four more followed me.

Talk about polluting the valley with cars idling waiting
for these foolish lights to change. If nothing changes
and they bring in this red-light law, it is a cash cow
for the city because we are all guilty doing this
and we will continue, I'm sure.
It's human nature.

In the Car Wash

In the car wash
water-feathers swoop and sweep
then splats of blue stuff,
then splats of pink stuff,
then the going-over with the protectant —
then the whumping of the dryers
scattering sideways froth & bubbles
as if parting the sheer curtain that divides us

& in the car wash's various illuminations
and showerings from up above & sideways
I'm reading Thomas Merton's little chapter
on "Silence"—opened at random—and "Silence"
isn't about silence at all but about nature.

When the great door lifts and the light goes green
we emerge — my car, my self, & the thoughts of Thomas
    Merton —
into an alley with winter weeds and branches
pressing hard against a fence as each clean car appears
with its happy occupant, its shining force.

Peak Oil

> *Got a new car, can't go very far*
> *Can't get to no Norway, can't get to Dakkar*

Need a new kind of gas, a new way of living
Won't go to New Brunswick, won't mind all the quibbling

About buses and bicycles, schedules so cruel
We wait in the rain till our shoes are in pools

Won't use any oil, can't use any gas
Just use and lose our corn, wheat, and grass!

> *Got a new car, can't go very far*
> *& taking the bus*
> *doesn't do very much!*

You can yell all you want, you can shop at the Bay
You can think it all through but it won't be okay

Cry as we want to, much as we think
We'll be stuck on the highway, wearing our mink!

> *Got a new car, got a new car*
> *Can't get very far, can't go to Dakar*

Won't go to New Brunswick, can't go to New York
Won't go to no Highlands, can't get to East Cork

Can't go to no Chile, can't go to Iran
Can't go to Australia, nobody can!

> *Got a new car, got a new car*
> *Can't get to no England, can't get to the bar*

We'll sing heartfelt anthems, we'll stand on our head
For principles, ethics, and life without lead

We need some new actions, new thoughts and clean skies
We need some fresh traction, new ways to get high!

> *Got a new car, got a new car*
> *Can't get to New Canaan, let alone Myanmar*

There are new kinds of gasses, made from cow's asses,
Methane, urethane, fields of sweet grasses

Cow patties, wind willows, large trees and small
Will give up the ghost to stand in a stall

And crowd and deliver and squeeze and release
The gas that we'll need to keep paying the lease

On earth's kind installments. For us and the rest
Have just about had it, we're so far in debts

> *And taking the bus*
> *Doesn't do very much*

So leave it to Hegel, leave it to Keats
Farewell sweet autumn, farewell sweet cheeks
Of halibut, cod, and German white wine,
We'll leave you the bill for such a good time!

(Got a fast track goin', a spondee showin',
A vittle, a tottle, and bag and a bottle. A nick
And a scratch, a poke and a smack — the stuff's
Relaxin', I've started hummin', I'm in the grooves,
I'm shakin' my hooves!)

> *A new kind of a car, a new kind of car*
> *Might get to New Orleans, might save Kandahar*

Might get us asking, what's the good
Of having a bookstore, of having a 'hood

We'd better start soon, we'd better not fail
To give it our best and not leave a trail
Of Timbits and corn chips and concrete and rust
And mountains of plastic that won't turn to dust
We'd better get ready, when Peak Oil comes
To be wearing our runners and swallowing Tums

> *For taking the bus*
> *Doesn't do very much*

Can't go to the mall, can't go to the temple,
Can't go to no classes, can't even go mental!

> *Got a new car, got a new car*
> *Can't go very far, go very far.*

Anonymous

for Renita

I could see there was something wrong with the way I had spelled
the word "anonymous." And later, at 12:30, showed up at the Mexican cafe
to find it closed though the website said "open today."

I wasn't the only one: an elderly couple
similarly confused, picked their way back
across the slush to their spattered vehicle so recently parked.

My friend arrived and seeing me waiting
on the sidewalk divined the situation.
We went to the Japanese restaurant a few doors down instead.

We talked about everything though our subjects were few.
The green tea took forever to steep. There were no leaves left
in our cups by which to tell the future.

We each had forgotten — momentarily — certain names,
certain plans. Plans that had to be altered, and plans
that were just thoughts, fantasies.

I was seeing myself in Albuquerque, or on Haida Gwaii,
— neither is easy to spell. My friend worries
about her old dog who needs to go out three times a night.

As it is, we live by a lake and are not lacking.
Quail rush across the driveway amid terror and cluck.
I thought I heard a bird today — the kind you hear in spring —
but isn't it too soon? Better to hang back until the coast is
   clear.

I Thought of Shelley

Half the summer reading Richard Holmes' biography
& feeling at times judgemental about Shelley's

"free love," a term I hadn't heard since the '60s.
Shelley used it, maybe coined it,

bent to live it. As bill bissett would say,
great for some, not so great for others.

Shadows fell, the sea later on was wild
though Shelley refused to take his sails down,
rescuers pleading with him through a speaking-trumpet.
"No!" they heard him shrieking over the wind,
— "shrieking": is it fair to take the shrillness
of his voice to that negation?

All three — Shelley and his crew of two —
went down with the *Don Juan,*
the title of Byron's hit poem

synecdoche for love freely given
in sloshing Venetian palaces
with women procured by Byron's gondolier
and countesses smelling of garlic

which Shelley found revolting,
and the Bridge of Sighs
an abomination.

The War Against the Imagination

notes from Creative Writing

The narrator doesn't seem at all like the sort of person who would kneel at his wife's commemorative bench in Stanley Park.

I didn't pick up on the fact that the narrator was a doll until close to the last page.

Maybe some of the leprechaun dialogue could be replaced?

I was following this poem until I got to the part about the slashed melon.

Could you be more specific about the "foreign-appearing" bra?

Are zombies that interested in whether the people they eat are attractive?

Do ignorant murderous people have to speak with a Southern US accent?

Again, the feeling is paramount but the circumstances vague.

Are you saying something about the way academics deal with myth?

Goosebumps march?

Too many hims and hers, plus the dog.

A story is just a small patch of time in a larger field of action.

The Suez Canal, rubies, people getting killed, explosions, guys stealing a boat — lots of drama and action!

The red hair is a good detail but I would like to see more of her appearance and witness more of her quirks.

What sort of expensive drinks?

Could it start at the hospital?

I'm thinking Sammy should be getting on your nerves earlier in the piece.

People just don't talk like that, even on Mars!

You portray Phil's dilemma quite vividly.

I sense the speaker's pain and frustration, but I'm not sure what exactly the speaker is describing.

Maybe the nurse needs to be softened up a bit by the stranger — lied to, whatever.

"Camping" is quite well written.

"Booze Cruise": Good narrative poem. "Impediments": good list poem.

Is this a ball of Wensleydale cheese that the moon resembles?

The hug scene at the end left me unconvinced. Richard is dead, so is the conceited liar. Love the one you're with?

I love the pine cone image at the end.

I enjoyed the description of the descent to the dungeon, the fat man's difficulties with it.

I confess the situations reminded me of those in soap operas, but maybe life is more like a soap opera than we'd like to think!

"Ivan the Terrible" is a terrific story — or beginning of a story, or a sketch, or a sort of micro-fiction.

And then there is the serum from two years ago that caused Tara to kill twelve people with her bare hands.

I cared about Ting and her trying to be ever more perfect.

I like this sense of a homicidal other lurking about any person, presumably.

Some of the setting details could be more pungent, especially when it comes to dead bodies lying all over the streets.

Not sure what is meant by "congelations" but it's a nice word! It might help if you were to read Ch. 10 about what is involved in writing dramatic scripts.

Is it possible the vacation is glossed over a bit too much?

Is it the first time the Roses have tormented Mr. Corbin?

"Falling fireball" for the sunset is quite effective.

MY EDUCATION AS A POET

Vernon, 1954

He worked for the city & early one spring morning
still dark out, he took me with him
to collect the still-burning oil lamps
from the road construction & put them in the back of the
    truck.
Still burning? Or extinguished, I don't recall

— and the privilege I felt, wordless in the front seat,
sitting still, being good
to deserve this honour, to be woken and taken out
so early with no one around but us

as he gathered the heavy sooty lamps
that guarded during the night the still-soft asphalt
of repaired pot-holes and altered curbs.

At My Mother's in Prince George

The river runs by so quietly
you'd fall into it if you were blind or daydreaming,
its path so deeply scored

so unimpeded by rock or shoal
it fails to sing
or splash but only proceeds

in the one clear direction, south I guess,
though it may at times diverge
as the bending valleys pull it onward

through canyons and underneath bridges
where a bright bush adorns a gravelly edge
people once sat on, thinking about something

as I do in my mother's guest room's
1940's honeymoon bedroom suite, thick maple
bedframe, dressing table with photos propped

on a beige linen runner.
Old brushes and combs.
A mirror with a long handle.

*

My mother and I watch TV,
eat our small supper.

"You're so smart, dear," she says,
"you should be on *Jeopardy!*"

The winning contestant loses all her prize money
with a wrong answer but clearly
has learned the protocol:

No crying or whining!
No gloating either, when it's the other guy
standing there with nothing all of a sudden.

The new categories are revealed with a flourish.
We top up our glasses with Mom's home-made Shiraz.
The three contestants look calm behind their pulpits.

*

Tonight's chamber concert is titled "Waning Crescent"
for the type of moon it is this night. Among other pieces
Mozart's "The Hunt" from the Haydn Quartets
will be performed at the Lutheran Church with
its austere altar & fine acoustics. The oboist is from Portugal.

It was beautiful but
driving around in the pitch dark afterwards
feeling old and diminished in capacities,
powerless and lonely in my mother's car

trying to read the street signs, pretending
to know where I'm going, the guy behind me
pushing with high-beams on

near where big dim houses twinkle on a far hillside
way beyond my ken, I don't know this place very well

anymore and I got turned around exiting the Lutheran
   Church
parking lot where the outside lights weren't working and
a fellow with a flashlight was motioning this way, this way

   *

It's nearing the end of hunting season.
Pickups have been through the car wash & sedans
contain more customers going to Seniors Day at the pharmacy
than camouflage-clad customers
surveying the parking lot in their rear-view mirror

Inside the pharmacy, swift and busy dispensing of tablets and
   instructions

I'm holding a form & when my name is called, I rise with
   alacrity,
I can hear alright, I can get out of here,
just an errand for my mother, not me, not yet

   *

The concert-master announced that Mozart's "The Hunt"
wasn't really about a hunt. It was just a name it
ended up with because of the prominence of horns.
I'm not alone though I'm alone here.
I worry about my mother, who's 90 and having trouble.
A tree seems to agree with me
when I think one of us should move up here
for a while. I think of all those I know with faraway mothers,
one in South Africa, several in England. Prince George
isn't that far but by now, my carry-on
is bulging and heavy, zipped up, the handle extended.

A huntress kneels in the night sky
drawing an arrow from her quiver. A carved wooden bear is
    standing up
at the Arrivals entrance at the airport, looking like a man
in a bear suit, which is what a bear is
in the occlusion of the waning crescent —
truth so modestly, so hilariously hidden
and present in the painted fur and long claws
of our disguises. The shuttle arrives at 4:40 a.m.,
stars still out, the other passengers
mute shapes looking out the window
at nothing, the odd building with lights on,
or just darkness going by, already gone.

Talking to My Mother on the Phone

We go over a few things, the weather, her cough
& energy, how long it has been since she's been out of the
    house.

She doesn't sound terrible and I have a couple of questions
about when she was in Tranquille Sanatorium and shared a
    room

with others. I was wondering if her friend from Masset
was her roommate, if you can call it that jaunty a thing,

but it wasn't her. She's still alive, Mom said. It was another
    girl,
very beautiful, who was a Christian Scientist

and refused the treatments. Then what was she doing in the
    hospital,
I asked. My mother said, she had TB. And what happened to
    her
was that she died.

What a tragedy, we agreed. But then, it was her belief
and she died in that belief, so who knows,

maybe she is better off, since she could very well have died
anyway, with the treatments or in spite of the treatments

and against her religion. I hope so, said my mother.
It was so sad because she was so beautiful, so young.

The doctors and nurses, her friends, and even my mother
must have tried to convince her; her family and the minister

at her other ear with their encompassing energy & certainty
about what disease was and how she could be helped.

Encompassing of nature, mind, God, imagination, spirit,
hope, faith, love. Who knows, my mother and I said,
maybe she was cured, even though she died.

Auntie Eileen

I was going to tell the story my mother told me about her Aunt Eileen. Auntie Eileen, who had the most beautiful red hair, left her husband and five children on a chicken farm in Chilliwack, BC, to run off with the Australian hired hand, had three more children with him in Perth, and returned to Canada in her seventies for a famous reunion with the five previous children, not one of whom bore her any ill will.

More than once her husband had tied Auntie Eileen up and locked her in the chicken coop, according to my mother. My mother, like Eileen, had grown up in Masset, BC, a three-days journey north and west from Chilliwack, free beside the ocean in fresh salty air. What on earth had led Eileen to live on a farm, let alone to having five children with a man who would treat her so badly? The rain pouring down and nowhere for her to go; chickens lined up in cages, laying eggs and awaiting execution. As my mother said, Eileen took off and left those kids behind so she must have been desperate. Eileen was lucky she and the hired hand made it all the way to Perth, Australia. Auntie Eileen could never let anyone know where she had gone, or her husband would have come after her and killed her.

There was Auntie Eileen, Auntie Phyllis, and Auntie Kathleen. Auntie Phyllis stayed in Masset with her husband Clarence, a pious Anglican. Auntie Kathleen married an American and moved to Portland, Oregon. One summer, around 1958 when I was 11 or 12, we drove to Portland to visit Auntie Kathleen. We slept in feather beds and in the morning were served poached eggs on beautiful china in a sunlit breakfast room. We went out for a walk one day and when Auntie Kathleen noticed a Black family walking toward us on the sidewalk, she made us cross to the other side of the street. I felt really bad about that, the realness of what she did and made us do to those people who were just going about their lives.

While at Auntie Kathleen's I read about a dozen Hardy Boys mysteries. Matthew, their grandson, owned the entire set. I guess that's about all I did during that visit — read Hardy Boys and study the staircase, the bedspreads, the leaded glass window panes, Matthew's demeanour. Matthew liked me. This made me feel excited and weird.

So what about the story of Auntie Eileen? I keep thinking about the part where Auntie Eileen is sneaking away from the chicken farm with her Australian lover, desperate, grieving, and terrified. Then making it all the way to Vancouver or Seattle to catch the boat with only the clothes on her back, the way Maggie Lloyd in Ethel Wilson's novel *Swamp Angel* walks out the kitchen door while supper is cooking and her husband has just taken off his coat and sat down at the dining room table. Why does a certain kind of imaginary woman always have the name "Maggie"? Illicit sorts of women who walk around their apartment wearing a slip and smoking a cigarette. According to my mother, Auntie Eileen was a sweet, good woman with the most beautiful red hair.

It was a different world in Maggie's day, in Auntie Eileen's day. You could know things by the outline of them, the way film noir will use a black cat, a hatted head, a paunch, or the shape of a revolver as a shadow on the wall. A frightened woman in an evening gown fainting. The sharp jut of a jaw beneath a fedora, the jangle of a telephone.

At first, I wanted to tell Auntie Eileen's story but what about Auntie Eileen's Australian lover? Let's say his name was

Philip and he was born in Brisbane. His family moved west to Perth when his father was transferred. Phil didn't do all that well in school, so he quit at age sixteen and started working as a cabin boy on the *Aorangi*, crossing the Pacific. His favourite port of call was Vancouver, BC, and he vowed to one day live there. How he wound up as a worker on a chicken farm in Chilliwack, who knows. That part of it is Phil's story alone, one entrusted, perhaps, only to Auntie Eileen.

Today, the outlines are not clear at all; in fact, one cannot, and should not, tell anything, any sort of story, from appearances. The sound of a story's appearances may be hiding a fact, or many facts. My story about Auntie Eileen has been disturbed, and I feel guilty about the tone I've used to tell it, without much feeling, after hearing it so often from my mother. Anyone's dream of escape can become anyone else's.

I was lately told by another, more distant, relative what in fact had happened to Auntie Eileen. To begin with, her name was Aileen, not Eileen; and she had blond hair, not red hair. The red hair, which was actually more of an auburn, belonged to Auntie Kathleen. Aileen's husband owned a farm in Langley, BC, not Chilliwack. He was horrible to Aileen and one night locked her in the barn, naked. She was rescued by a neighbour, but her husband, let's call him Howard, refused to let her back into the house and shortly afterward told their four, not five, children (two girls and two boys) that she had died. She in fact had returned to Masset to live with her parents; a visit that lasted six years. It was decades later, after she had moved to Mt. Isa, an Australian mining town, that the children who thought she was dead found out she was alive and that she had had two more daughters.

Auntie Aileen was a sweet and docile person. In a childhood portrait, Aileen and Kathleen are youngsters in hair-bows and smocked dresses, Kathleen smiling confidently and Aileen shy and soft beside her. This is because, according to my confidante, Aileen had contracted encephalitis at age three and after that had remained "slow"; and that this slowness aggravated Howard. Now the picture of Auntie Aileen changes again. A husband constantly aggravated; a husband whose own mother, by the way, was "insane." A husband who told his children their mother had died, when she hadn't. Had there been a pretend funeral, phony grieving (on his part), a fake headstone? More likely it was something like, "your mother is dead and so she won't be mentioned again."

How terrified Aileen must have been, that she lived for the next six years in the same province and never once returned to Langley. What conversations had she had with her family in Masset about the fate of her children? Why didn't anyone do anything? Perhaps because Aileen was slow, and vulnerable, and it was thought imprudent, or a hopeless case. And because it would have been a terrible shock to the children had Aileen showed up alive after all.

My mother's Auntie Aileen. My own great-aunt Aileen.

When Auntie Aileen decided to go to Australia it was not with our imagined Philip but with a Londoner on his way to Australia the long way around. Maybe she left without telling anyone, and this was the "running off with" part of the story that my mother remembered. Or maybe they all decided it was fine; that this way, it would be easier, for the next while at least, for Aileen to put the Langley business behind her. To forget, and to be forgotten.

Uncle Dave

Uncle Dave was driving us somewhere and the next thing we knew we were in the ditch, with the sun shining silently all around us. Someone must have stopped and helped. Uncle Dave was further mortified by having a wooden leg, his own lost to diabetes some years before. Dave was a big man, a nice man, but I imagine there was hell to pay for my little brother, who from the back seat had put his hands tightly over Dave's eyes, so he couldn't see and crashed the car and we all could've been killed.

In fact, that may have been the last straw for Dave and his wife, our aunt Jessie. They had kindly taken in my 4-year-old brother and me after our mother was admitted to the TB sanatorium in Kamloops, BC. Aunt Jessie and Uncle Dave lived in a flat and featureless landscape somewhere in Alberta. The previous child-care arrangement our dad scrounged up hadn't worked out — the babysitter drank and had her boyfriend over all the time — so Jessie and Dave stepped forward to help out. Our dad stayed near his job at an oil refinery near Tranquille Sanatorium in the hot, dry BC Interior, while my brother and I tried to fit in to our cousins' small house. I don't think the arrangement lasted very long. The hands-over-the-eyes business was bad enough, but it was also that it was just too much, a seven year old and a four year old suddenly joining someone's family. Jessie wasn't happy about it, which I was painfully aware of. I tried to stay out of her way, but that only angered her further. She'd get mad at me for hanging around outside on the swing after she'd called us in for supper twice already. "Get in here now!" she would say from inside the screen door.

But the really great thing that happened while we were there is that Uncle Dave took me to a movie in town one afternoon. This was the first movie I had ever seen. Over the passing years, I often wondered if what I remembered most vividly from that movie — a woman swimming in a large glassed-in tank, and the glass breaking and the water, and the woman, pouring out — really happened. I also remembered scenes, preceding the catastrophe, of the woman just swimming around underwater, in this sort of human aquarium, as a form of nightclub entertainment. It turns out that the movie was called *Million Dollar Mermaid* and starred Esther Williams as the Australian swimming sensation Annette Kellerman, who was notorious for wearing a one-piece bathing suit back in whatever year it was she decided to jump off the ship she was on and swim the rest of the way across the English Channel. Later on, she swam in glass tanks in solo and synchronized swimming displays, and one day one of the tanks did shatter, causing a spinal injury that ended Kellerman's career. The movie also boasted extravagant over-the-top Busby Berkeley kaleidoscopic aquatic productions, all pinks and greens with humming voices breaking into ecstasies of soothing excitement, adding enchantment to the plot. Of all the things that happened during those years, I'll never forget Uncle Dave's kindness in taking the trouble, what with his wooden leg, his crashed car, and his stressed-out wife, to take me with him to see *Million Dollar Mermaid*, and get us out of the house for a while.

Pleasant St.

This time, we were moving into town. Usually, we moved within the vicinity of Brocklehurst, most recently to a rancher at the end of a long driveway, near the sawmill. This is where I chewed my nails reading Bobbsey Twins mysteries. Another mystery was my best friend Roberleigh. Her parents were health nuts from California. Everyone wondered what they were doing living in the rural outskirts of North Kamloops. Maybe they were Communists or worshipped a strange religion. Her father would do sit-ups on a slant board, twisting his torso this way and that, with his dark mustache and white undershirt.

Now we were moving to Pleasant St., to a two-storey house in a residential neighbourhood in town. This was the closest we had ever come to a white-picket-fence sort of life. Dad had become an Electrolux vacuum cleaner salesman, and while driving around would come across situations he could help out with. One was a litter of puppies, from which he chose the cutest. Another was a fellow Dad picked up hitchhiking. He was moved to pity by the Norwegian's story of immigration and bad luck, and brought him home to stay with us until he got on his feet. Dad, being of Norwegian descent, still knew enough of the language to communicate with this man, let's call him Karl, about basic things — but then, language being language, nothing ever remains very basic. Maybe Dad and Karl shared an outlook on life that was familiar both existentially (on the brink of total disaster) and emotionally (brooding, tender-hearted).

Dad enjoyed demonstrating the Electrolux at home. He'd scatter a good quantity of the special demo-dirt over the clean floor and suck it up instantly with the hose attachment. The Electrolux left a pleasant eucalyptus scent wherever it went; its canister was a rich dark brown; the noise of its motor and rolling wheels elegantly subdued.

It was following a day of Electrolux demonstrations that Dad came home with Ruby. I don't know whether Dad picked her up hitchhiking or was in some other way delegated to bring her to our place. She was seventeen and pregnant and probably her parents had kicked her out of the house. It was decided that it would be okay if Ruby shared my bed, so there we were, she on the left, me on the right. I remember her wearing a green maternity top. Ruby in the green maternity top, Ruby crying, Ruby's big stomach sticking out. But most vivid and fascinating was the drama of Ruby talking in a smothered voice on the hallway telephone. That was when the larger social impact of her condition registered on me. Ruby really was in trouble. A spot in a Home for Unwed Mothers would have been waiting for her and for the baby she'd give up for adoption, but I didn't know that then.

I went to a nice red-brick school close to downtown, and I was signed up for Brownies even though the Brownie ethos was foreign to me, the orderliness, the assumption that knot-tying and spool-knitting would be attentively supervised at home. Instead, my best friend Kathleen and I spent many hours together reading love comics and movie-star magazines over at her place. We savoured the large tears and black tresses and sobbing sensuous mouths of *Modern Love* and studied in the pages of *Photoplay* the perfections of Audrey Hepburn and Doris Day. We had to keep our voices down, though, because Kathleen's mom was always in bed. We'd tiptoe downstairs past the darkened bedroom where you could see the shape of someone under the blankets. I wondered about it, but I never asked Kathleen why her mother slept all day. We just always had to be quiet. One afternoon, Kathleen's mom was up, cheerful and busy, and she made us scads of cinnamon toast while she went in and out to the back porch to hang the washing on the line. She kept making the toast and we kept eating it, and eating it, and eating it. It was good, made from the bread her dad would bring home from the bakery he worked at — her dad, who I remember as wearing a large white apron and having something wrong with his eyes.

Churchgoing

She'd scooted over so quickly I didn't see her at first, but then, sure enough, it was her, ready with her hand to take mine during the upcoming Lord's Prayer. I wasn't a Lord's Prayer hand-holder, but what could I do now, there were only the two of us in the pew. I caught a glimpse of a black coat or jacket. I didn't associate the color black with her — she was more a red type. Perhaps she was shrinking. Her husband was wearing photochromic glasses and had been reading the first scripture, the Old Testament one. He pronounced "Ezra" "Erra" and actually skipped a line and a half. I had been reading along in the missal; otherwise I probably would have noticed only a syntactical slip. I hoped I didn't look too annoyed.

For years, this couple had been getting on my nerves, with their ostentatious "amens." Were they really that overjoyed and religious? Was I just envious of their exemplary coupledom, glued together in the third pew? They reminded me of the Pentecostals who ran the Daily Vacation Bible School my brother and I were sent to in the summertime. DVBS was the perfect way to get your kids off your hands: it was free, it was "religious," and they had their own door-to-door bus service. We would spend mornings doing bible-related crafts and reciting the verses we'd had to memorize the night before. *For by his stripes ye shall be healed.* During the afternoon sermons, Holy Rollers would work themselves up into spasms and shouts. It was mostly men and I wonder now what they were doing on weekday afternoons twitching and writhing at the Temple, as it was called.

The bus pulled up, we got on with our homework assignment and our craft of the day (a plaque) and were returned to the stifling little house in Brocklehurst where our mother stood at the woodstove canning tomatoes. *God Is Love*, said the plaque, the words affixed to a crumpled-up tinfoil background. Our baby sister was asleep, so we'd go back outside and ride our bikes around for a while.

Another Poem for My Mother

For the required length of time I enjoyed
the waters of life, amniotic,
ancestral, living close to Old Masset
in my mother's body. Scared with her friend to go look in the
    trees
where Haida interred their dead, it was said,
along with their jewels, bracelets, and combs,
or on the barge *The Bobolink* taking supplies to Langara Island
& the long-bearded fishermen who lashed whales as ballast
to the sides of their boats.

On the barge we floated past dead towns
of a northern jungle.

> (Do you love me Dogfish Mother?
> Whose eye, whose tooth implanted in your fin?
> Your grin a gate of knives, your crown two long-
>   beak birds,
> your sad face at the end of a line.)

Billows & tides, storms, depths, surfaces always in motion,
always changing.
And she, a fish out of water in the broiling interior hinterland
of Tranquille Sanatorium, age 27.

What is nature?
Where is mother?
Who is Sue Halpern? Did she not write a book? A book
oft cited at Davos (formerly Berghof Schatzalp Sanatorium,
so high on the mountaintop
that in winter they had to bring the dead down
on bobsleds). Where the gold cure was popular.
Where my mother's stepfather went for treatments
and returned cured, for a while, to Masset, and played the
   violin,
and took his little step-daughter,
my mother, out with him on *The Bobolink*.

The Oddness of Elegy

My father died twenty years ago today as my mother
reminded me on the phone & I thought
yes, he'd been on my mind — the mind of me
who doesn't remember anniversaries
the way my husband does — the date my husband arrived
in Canada, the day of his mother's birth, his father's death,
his grand-niece's birthday which falls on New Year's Eve —
and how old so-and-so would be now, had he or she lived,
94 in my own father's case. He could still be alive
if he hadn't died! My husband's father would be 103
if he hadn't died either, of a heart attack at age 43,
but in those days they couldn't save people the way
they do now, plus he had passed away in the middle of
the night and it was his wife, my husband's mother,
who to her horror found him dead beside her in
the morning. My husband said he remembered how odd
it was to hear the doctor's voice so early in the morning,
in the house. I walked today as I usually do,
with the dog, along a lakeside path, imagining my father
"up there" — that one day we might meet again,
as promised. Would we be
balls of light or flickering flashes or
nothing except some sort of knowing? We would shed
tears of joy and the tears of sorrow would be wiped away.
Do you still see me from up there? Who are you
when you appear in my dream as you did not long ago,
fully yourself? The lake gleams in its winter opalescence,

subtle and heavy, & the dog and I turn around at the
usual spot and rejoin the path, the marks
of our feet backward now and the old landmarks
reappearing on the left.

My Education as a Poet

> 'Where affliction conquers us with
> brute force, beauty sneaks in and
> topples the empire of the self from
> within.'
>
> — SIMONE WEIL

(Dad, I dreamed about you last night. Mom showed me your
stiff hand open at the top of the bed and said "See?" I had to
agree it was stiff and dead alright. And I was freaking out
because I'd missed a meeting at work, and so was relieved
Dad had died because I'd have an excuse. But then he returns,
is walking around like nothing happened though he looks
pale and frail and soon to die again, possibly). He would sing,

Go to sleep my little pickaninny
Underneath the silver shiny moon
Hushabye, lullaby, mama's little baby

and before that my grandmother's coral brooch —
Grandma: pianist, good-time girl, Rosicrucian —
the brooch I lost one night at one of those parties
it took days to recover from, beating myself up —
the good lickins with wooden spoon with branch from Sacred
    Grove
with belt with whatever was to hand & we were lucky
because when the kids down the street were bad

they had to go find and present to their mom
their own stick for the good lickins they got at the Shuswap

their dad would walk out
into the lake holding up a bottle
in one hand, a glass in the other, and hoist himself up
onto the raft, us on the beach
laughing & waving, he was an okay guy,
a great joke teller, I'd always listen hard from
the bedroom when I heard Bill's ice cubes quieten down
& he'd say "A Jew and a Catholic
walk into a bar" but even better were the mysterious
sayings that would emerge out of fairly long periods
of stupefied silence at 3:30 in the morning
and the laughter was tired or maybe
there was some sort of decorum such as when
someone would leap across the living room
to light his wife's cigarette, he was so in love with her
my mother said, she'd barely have the cigarette
out of the package before he'd be over there with the lighter.
Poetry: a bright flame.
I always knew we were in for a long night
when Dad got out the banjo and ripped into "Bye Bye Blues"
& who knew how the evening would turn out,
in joy or in sorrow.

Sometimes the parties would take place at Bill's or
somewhere else in which case there might be a phone call
at 4 a.m. to come and drive them home even though I couldn't
drive yet so I'd walk over and get the keys,
just put it in drive, Dad would say, & off we'd go
with the high beams on & the birds beginning to tweet.
Brett Enemark used to say this was Young Driver Training
in Prince George; he'd done it, too. At least they were being

responsible by not getting behind the wheel in a condition
Mom referred to as "tight". This was poetry: terms like
getting tight.

Both Bill and Dad were good joke-tellers but Dad,
a big fan of Bob Hope, had a more technical approach.
He'd study Hope's routine on the *Ed Sullivan Show*.
"Listen to this" he'd say, as we scrutinized the timing.
Dad could even imitate Bob Hope's little smile.
Poetry: timing, a little smile.
And the lyrics to "Ragtime Cowboy Joe":
"He's a high-falutin', rootin' tootin', son of a gun
from Arizona . . ." Dad would finish
with a flourish of his pick hand, whirling it around
like a pitcher on the mound, and give his little grin and
shake his head as if to say, Boy, that was fun! And reach
for his topped-up Bacardi.

He transferred mandolin-type playing to the banjo &
    worshipped
the guitar moves of Les Paul. I can still hear the wall-of-sound
playing and singing, a drone poured off the surface
of the tight harmony with Mary Ford. "The World is Waiting
for the Sunrise" was Dad's most soulful cover —
you'd hear him practicing in the basement with the tiki lights
    on
over the dark little bar.

Before that, in Kamloops, when grandma's piano arrived
after her death Dad drove me over the bridge for lessons.
My first piece was called "Indian Dance", a steady
single-note repetition on the left hand and a simple
two-note slightly sad yet menacing-sounding melody on the
    right.

Poetry: something out of whack. Grandma had played that
 same piano
for friends and guests both whites and Haida thirty years
 before
in Masset, accompanied on violin by her husband Edward.
It was known that in the hands of certain women, red cedar
 bark could be pounded to a softness greater than cashmere.
 But most of those women if not all of them were dead by
 then. Most of the artists, carvers, and poets were dead by
 then also, or crippled by disease.
Mom's bio-dad, an O'Donnell, logging accountant and
 charmer,
disappeared and was heard to have died on the *Queen Mary*.
Her grandfather James Martin was then
her father until he died when she was seven, and then
tubercular Edward arrived from Germany with his violin and
 soon
he died too. Poetry: consumption and epitaph.

Mom would be homesick for the sound
of the canneries and salty crashing ocean,
kelp and sand dunes north of Masset
toward Rose Spit where Raven discovered Humans.
Every Christmas a dozen cans of Alaska King crabmeat
would arrive from what she called The Islands.
She'd tumbled down the white dunes & gone out after storms
with a can opener to see what had washed up from
 shipwrecks:
mostly pork and beans. Poetry: a can opener. Treasures
were the glass buoys — large, pocked, thick-glassed orbs
from Japanese fishing fleets out somewhere in the
four thousand miles of open sea to the west of Rose Spit.
In the sanatorium Mom was homesick for fresh fish,
she and her friend from The Islands both at death's door

in young womanhood with children at home later sent
Haida bracelets for Xmas — mine was Dogfish Woman
crafted by someone whose signature was "XX" and
whose carving was a bit off on an angle. Poetry:
off on an angle amidst the TB and the whalers and the
   moieties.

AROUND THEN

Anna Akhmatova

> *I cannot tell if the day*
> *is ending, or the world, or if*
> *the secret of secrets is inside me again.*

Anna Akhmatova
with a black shawl
and a great nose that said, I am a living poet

Joseph Brodsky knew her
& the mystics and philosophers,
psychiatrists and economists
around then but for a long time before that
companions had died from gulag or suicide,
herself with typhus, TB —

In a long lineup trying to see
through the crowded gate and into the political prison
where her son, or another one loved was being held

with food for him anxious in the pocket of her coat

a sad exhausted woman standing there also
asked her, "Can you describe this?" and Akhmatova said
"Yes I can," and the woman smiled.

For years, her poems were recited secretly among friends.
Or she would write one out on a scrap of paper, quickly, let

her visitor read it and then burn it — "Hands, matches, an ashtray.
A ritual beautiful & bitter."

Four Books Side by Side on the Shelf

1. ALICE NOTLEY & DOUGLAS OLIVER, *The Scarlet Cabinet*

This large, suggestive, Hawthornian volume in a plain red cover is about women and men, dreams and books, memories, fantasies, language, apparitions, voices, and other personal and erotic curiosities. It reminds me to go everywhere and to use everything. It sees poetry everywhere, as some might the presence of God. And it reminds me that the vagina is a big yet small important thing. And that there are cabinets for every and any sort of collection. And that no one has ever gone without poetry, as Notley insists when, in "Descent of Alette" and other poems, any and all idiomatic groupings of words appear in quotation marks.

I met Alice Notley at a workshop at the Kootenay School of Writing in Vancouver. She is a dear, inspiring figure. She was a big dreamer; she grew up in Needles, California. She, desert; me, Kamloops: similar thing. I imagine a similar small town, a daily wind, a spaciousness. I feel similar to Alice Notley in our colouring: dark hair, fair skin. And Alice's choice of husbands was commendable. Both their sad and tragic deaths deprived her of an essential companionship if one is to be everywhere and everyday in writing poetry.

"We need your words," Alice said to the poets assembled in the room. We wrote on our laps and read aloud the results. Everyone's was amazingly different.

2. EDNA O'BRIEN, *Lantern Slides*

Edna O'Brien and I are alike in our colouring: dark hair, fair skin; and in her and my case, eyes that tilt downward at the outer corners. I imagine Edna O'Brien as a bit of a handful. I would love to listen to her talking with her friends in a pub.

The voice in *Lantern Slides* (a book of short stories) is that of the exile telling about some all-too-familiar place where people think they are relatively unnoticed by others. Not so. This is the knowing voice of an everyone who surmises community secrets and whose conclusions may very well be accurate. This voice is relentlessly dedicated to staying outside, pitiless, hilarious, and borne along by the rhythms and idioms of the old place, the place where those whose miserable, deluded, and desperate lives are lived. One might say: the usual Irish fare of incestuous siblings, alcoholic priests, victimized women, poverty, and few pleasures (drinking, illicit sex, pickles eaten with white bread fresh from the bakery). Occasionally, visitors come to this village, rich women with "varnished nails and lizard purses."

Some of the stories are about those with the wherewithal to try to escape. They vacation in Mediterranean countries or settle for tacky and disappointing seashore hotels where the clientele most likely includes a family with twelve children or a lonely bachelor with poor hygiene.

This is the voice of my Irish relatives on my mother's side, the ones I never met. But my sentences and lines sometimes remember them, in certain constructions. Here is an Edna O'Brien sentence that I could have written the rhythm of: "Some go there, dally, and allow themselves to be hauled into thickets or bracken or verdure." The possibilities: "or". The violent gestures: "hauled". And this sentence, which delights me, about a gypsy woman who steals a pair of shoes —

brogues that their owner had just dyed dark brown and that were drying on the front step: "She was caught not long after, found by the sergeant at some sort of regatta where she was telling fortunes, squatting down on a bit of red velvet, giving the impression of an Eastern sage, and wearing the shoes."

3. RICHARD PALMER, *Hermeneutics*

Sometime in the mid-1980s, I typed a letter to an old friend from Simon Fraser University who was now living in Ottawa and writing text for the federal government's department of historical monuments. As I recall, I was replying to a letter he had written to me, and I mentioned that I'd been reading about hermeneutics and finding it quite interesting.

On the envelope of the letter he sent in reply was the following return address: "Herman Neutics." In the letter, he objected strenuously to the very notion of "hermeneutics," and he ended his piece with the dark reminder that "all is vanity."

To a historian, the idea that "all is vanity" must be obvious on a daily basis.

I think I must have read a fair chunk of Richard Palmer's book, *Hermeneutics*. When I look through it now, I see a generous and lucid critical intelligence at work. I suppose that's why I was so taken with it, made so happy by it, back in the mid-1980s. I'd have to go back and read it again, though, to see why; but I know I won't because it will have an antique and disorienting feeling that will remind me of those years and what I was looking for in Richard Palmer's book.

4. BERNARD LOVELL, *Emerging Cosmology*

Next door to Banyen Books, Vancouver's most successful New Age bookstore, was a natural foods restaurant where you'd serve yourself and then go sit at the counter at the window and read the free copy of *Common Ground* that came with your Banyen purchase. Let's say it was a Sunday afternoon in January. Rain skidded around on the hooded Gore-Tex jackets of passersby. In a perpetual-dusk miasma of lentil soup and grey traffic, I would ponder advertisements by too-good-looking men who would be happy to solve your sexual problems. Across the street were herbal apothecaries, alternative cancer centres, and natural foods emporiums stocked with barrels of mung beans and bins of steel-cut oats. I would have gotten Bernard Lovell's *Emerging Cosmology* on one of those Sundays. All of a sudden we're talking about resolvable stars, the boggling magnitude of the Milky Way, appalling globular-blobbed emptiness. Explosions like you wouldn't believe. Dead stars, black holes, dwarves. And it's all just out there, not far beyond the blue horizon.

Banyen carried the entire Bollingen series of the works of Carl Jung, the Koran, many translations of the Bible, many reassuring analyses of female malaise by Marie-Louise von Franz, the Whole Earth catalogues, and several editions of Richard Grossinger's *Planet Medicine*, a book full of human ideas never far from my reach even now.

The Pangs of Sunday

You'd go to Banyen Books on Sunday afternoons,
a searcher after meaning. So much meaning, so
little time! Was it to be mental or physical, your
ailment, in the end. In the end the ailment revolved
around love, mental or physical. Across the road
was the health food store, the herbalist, and the pains
and the ills of real estate & car insurance even though

it was a matter of proximity
and luck, how you arrived anywhere with no one
to witness and adjust, no one to drive the car. I
could get my fortune told in the sweet
cafe of Sunday by the woman with the bangle bracelets
and the low voice and the black, tangled hair — who else
to believe? — you only hoped your tip would be enough
to jumpstart the engine of your happy fate idling
while you got settled with your purse, etc.,
and turned up the volume on the radio.

Daphne In the Headphones

Sometime in the 1970s I transcribed a taped interview in which Daphne Marlatt spoke about writing, poetry, and language, perhaps in the first of her "Vancouver" poems. It may have been part of a project George Bowering had initiated and I believe the interview was part of a longer series. In those days at Simon Fraser University's English Department, faculty would just assume a graduate student would do specific tasks for them. It was part of your education. Even as an undergraduate I wrote a bibliography on Ezra Pound's music reviews; transcribed audiotapes of Charles Olson lecturing; transcribed a Jack Spicer notebook into typescript. Whoever else this particular project of George's may have involved, it was the interview with Daphne that I remember best.

I would be set up in one of the Department offices with a Dictaphone machine and a typewriter. You pressed the machine's pedal with your foot and typed along with the voice in the headset. To rewind, you pressed another pedal; likewise to fast-forward. By these means, Daphne's sentences would appear in typescript through my ears and hands and feet, an annunciation-like situation, intimate and magical, for who is who in such a situation. The transcriber is an instrument, not an intermediary. And now a number of things have just occurred to me. One is how much transcribing I've done, not only of voices and cadences and syntaxes like Daphne's, but also of the voices, cadences and syntaxes of various bosses at many secretarial jobs I had taken then, in the late '60s and into the '70s, when operating the Dictaphone also involved knowing how to fix sentences, even nuance, in one of the many letters informing someone that their insurance claim was being denied, or that they owed a certain amount of money, or that their desire for a pay raise was unwarranted.

Also occurring to me just now is that my father had been a Morse code operator for the Navy, a "telegrapher," as it says on his headstone, during the war years and for some years afterward. In the war years he had been stationed in Masset, BC, on what was then known as the Queen Charlotte Islands, to intercept Japanese code and send the decoded information to other telegraphers as far south as San Diego. After the war, he continued to work as a telegrapher — but also a photographer, an office typist, a door-to-door salesman for encyclopedias and vacuum cleaners, but it was the adventure of telegraphy that he enjoyed most. You never knew what was going to come across the wires. The worst experience was when he found himself tapping out the telegram that was informing his father that his mother had just died in the hospital, following vascular surgery.

Later, he had a fascination with the potential of reel-to-reel tape recorders. He would tape himself and various friends playing a piece of music like "Bye Bye Blackbird" and splice the results into impressive-sounding versions. He taped me speaking into the small beige grid of the microphone and played it back ("That's me?" "That's you!"); and he taped his own farts over a number of months, splicing them into one of Prime Minister Trudeau's speeches. Dad would also fool around with multiple tracks, splicing ukulele chords into tunes like "It's Crying Time Again" to express how he felt leaving the Maui Sands motel after a two-week vacation. In another life he might have continued working with sound technology and composition, or record production, instead of having to get up at 5:00 a.m. to fill furnace oil tanks on

40-below Prince George winter mornings. He loved to imitate ethnic "accents" when telling jokes, specializing in Jewish accents gleaned from TV comedians. When I think of it now, my particular "research assistant" skills were not without genetic nudging, nor the many projects since then that have involved bringing speech into print. Channeling Daphne in the early '70s was part of my education as a poet. The earlier part was my father's lifelong fascination with voice and rhythm.

Churchgoing (2)

An old woman near the front
prays with both hands over her face

a coral pink crocheted tam sits
at the back of her head, her too-large raincoat
navy blue

she prays and is the man
beside her, less frail, rosier,
husband, friend, or as they say
care-giver —

is she praying or just resting,
just fed up. Which is also
praying. Might he help her down
the stairs, do the driving?

He looks straight ahead, as if through
the altar and beyond. Perhaps she
hides tears. Perhaps she prays for him.

A Tourist Church in Drome–Provence

A young woman and a child of two or three
were squatting alongside a recently-covered grave.

The churchyard was otherwise deserted,
pea-gravel nicely raked right up to the lintel.

No footprints, not even the wind.

She pats and arranges the grave and the flowers,
the toddler holds onto the edge of a nearby tomb.
A cyclist had been killed not long ago in this region —
was it him? Her husband?

I tried to open the church door but before even trying
knew it was locked and empty, picturesque on the hill.

What saint or mystery had it consecrated? — and
perhaps still did in the raw sunshine and quietness.

The young woman didn't seem sad enough, we thought,
to have been so recently bereaved as this grave suggested

with fresh dark dirt still piled on top. After she left
we wanted to check the inscription on the gravestone
but didn't want her to see us
being curious about her visitation.

CHARLES, FRANCES, RALPH AND ME

Charles, Frances, Ralph, and Me

The recent fracas that followed an audience "question" about how Black Mountain College could call itself progressive when it was patriarchal, racist, and white (following a four-poet panel discussion at the Black Mountain College exhibit in Los Angeles), as well as my own very recent visit to the exhibit, has precipitated some memories and feelings about my long association with the late Ralph Maud as co-editor of the two editions of the correspondence between Charles Olson and Frances Boldereff. You might say "patriarchy" was the underlying theme, in both theory and practice, not only of the correspondence but also of Ralph's and my relationship as we slowly transcribed and published the letters. The bickering, the disputes, the discussions centred mostly on how "crazy" Boldereff was (Ralph) or why she may have, legitimately, felt Olson was exploiting her (me), mirroring uncomfortably Ralph's and my working arrangement.

Ralph always took Olson's side when it came to any problems between him and Frances, many stemming from the fact that Olson was married (first to Connie Olson, then to Betty Olson) during the most intense years of their love affair. Frances' most egregious and unforgivable acts, in Ralph's view, were when she got involved with a "beautiful young Negro" she'd met (*picked up*) on the subway and told Olson about; the other was when she wrote to mock Olson that she had found a man more "Maximus" than him.

Otherwise we were working out technical things — probable dates of undated letters; possible missing letters;

illegible handwriting; unknown references — which, when solved, caused us great satisfaction. I'd type the transcription for an hour or two each working session, then we'd have lunch and then maybe work for another half hour. We did enjoy the fraught and the unfraught times, both between Boldereff and Olson and between ourselves. Ralph was unhappy any time he thought I found any legitimacy at all in Boldereff's "demands," as Ralph called them, on Olson; and any time it seemed that I might be in agreement with Tom Clark about Boldereff in particular, or with any of his opinions about Olson.

For the most part I didn't — I was as put off by Clark's 1991 biography, *The Allegory of a Poet's Life*, as many readers were. But later on, I began to think more generously about what Clark may have been saying. This was confirmed a couple of years ago while reading Iain Sinclair's *American Smoke*, in which he writes "Clark is not composing a biography. He's attempting a fiction of history: large poet in small times, a culture that has no use for him." Ralph, as Olson's chief defender, was fact-checking every sentence Clark wrote to the point of actually proving the biography *was* fiction. Olson criticizing female students at Black Mountain College; Olson chasing woman X or Y around; Olson breaking John Wiener's heart by spiriting Panna Grady off to England for an abortion; Olson taking fistfuls of psilocybin mushrooms; Olson hitting a child with his car: all lies or distortions, as Ralph detailed in many issues of the *Minutes of the Charles Olson Society* newsletter. Clark's riposte was to republish the biography in 2000 with not a word changed. Ralph's riposte to that was his own 2008 "reactive biography," *Charles Olson at the Harbor*, which consolidates the anti-Clark research published in years of *Minutes* issues.

However, my big victory had been to persuade Ralph that Boldereff's side of the correspondence was worth transcribing in the first place. (Not that it would have gone unpublished for long.) One day in the middle of the 1980s Ralph phoned and asked me if I'd have a look at some materials he'd brought back from the University of Connecticut: a twenty-year correspondence between Charles Olson and the heretofore unknown Frances Boldereff. Ralph judged Frances's letters embarrassing and worthless, while Olson's would prove to be very useful to the fund of Olson scholarship. I was also being asked to "look at" the correspondence with a view to, possibly, transcribing Olson's side of it for publication. I was a lightning typist and had worked with Ralph before, while a student at SFU in the 1960s, and we had continued a friendship.

Unfortunately for Ralph, he had gotten the same answer (i.e., no) from another person he'd shown the correspondence to. But by then he had run out of options. I had the skills, the experience, and the basic knowledge of Olson's work to do the transcription. Plus, I was curious, and eager to delve into the scandal and energy of the letters. I would do the transcription, but it would have to be the whole thing, not just Olson's letters. What I didn't have, though, was a lot of spare time. The task seemed Herculean. There were nearly five hundred letters. And Ralph, being a patient scholar, was a stickler for detail. It took three decades for the entirety of the correspondence to be published; the first edition of the letters, *A Modern Correspondence* (truncated for the sake of length to the 1947–1950 period) wasn't published until 1999. But then, Ralph wasn't all that eager to spring crazy Frances onto the Olsonian deck; and I was, as Frances had been, a single working mother with many other ongoing projects and adventures.

Ralph would come over with the three-ring binders he used as a filing system for everything he was working on, including the *Minutes of the Charles Olson Society*. He would have arranged the letters in chronological order and I would transcribe one small batch of them at a time, with Ralph beside me proofing what was showing up on the computer screen. Olson's letters were typewritten to start with, but Frances's, being hand-written, were harder to decipher. Ralph insisted on including marginalia, envelope notes, telegrams, postmark details, and unsent letters in the final manuscript. But it was also fascinating material, fascinating to see their relationship unfolding, folding, and buckling under mythologized pressures (visualized gorily in Ken Warren's Jungian/anthropological fantasia in a *House Organ* review in 2000).

Ralph had taken very seriously Olson's request that he become Olson's "scholar". This had occurred at the 1963 Berkeley poetics conference. Featured poets were permitted to have their scholars accompany them (for free admission) to the various events. (I wonder who else's scholars were attending the conference, and who they were.) From then on, Ralph conscientiously fulfilled his role. Legendary is Ralph's patient replication of Olson's library in his own home in Vancouver; legendary also his patient pursuit of anyone who had been acquainted with Olson, including Frances Boldereff, whom he had visited at some point prior to my involvement with the correspondence. There were to be no more visits; I would now be the visitor/detective, since Frances had told Ralph not to come back.

When I finally met Frances a year or two after we began the transcription, she was eighty-six and in the beginnings of dementia. I'd gone all the way to Illinois, presented her with a bottle of Irish whisky, and settled in to talk. When I mentioned Charles Olson, she had no idea what I was talking about. Sometime the next day she said "Olson? I knew an Olson once." She complained that he ate her out of house and home; and how he gave her nothing back as a woman: "'I'm writing to her. What more does she want?'" What Frances really liked to talk about were the glories of the New York Public Library, where she had worked for a time and where she'd borrowed the Irish books and the volumes of Blake that began her research into *Finnegans Wake*. I visited Frances three times, once at her house in Woodward, Pennsylvania, where I also went in 2003 to attend her funeral; and twice at her home in Urbana, Illinois, where she lived with her husband, Thomas J. Phipps, Jr.

Ralph's role as Olson's scholar became seriously time-consuming when Tom Clark published *The Allegory of a Poet's Life*. No one's objections to it were as detailed as Ralph's. "Tawmmm Claaaark," Ralph would intone whenever he had occasion to mention his name. And if I ever preferred Frances's conduct to Olson's in the correspondence, or thought Frances was influential in the invention of Maximus, I'd be accused of being on the side of Tawmmm Claaaaark.

But I'd always thought Clark's respectful treatment of Frances Boldereff in the biography was immensely preferable to Ralph's denigrations and belittlements. Clark saw that Boldereff had played an essential and significant role in the development of Olson's poetics. To me also, working so closely with the "voice" of her letters, this was obvious. And it remains obvious to me, as it is to Clark, that Frances Boldereff was instrumental in the development of "projective verse" (the essay and the poetics) and in the generation of *The Maximus Poems*, not to mention the untold number of references and images gleaned from "his Muse" (as Clark refers to her) in many other poems including "In Cold Hell, In Thicket," "The Kingfishers," "For Sappho, Back," "La Chute," "The She-Bear," "Ode on Nativity," etc. Boldereff's leads, suggestions, and urgent recommendations (in conversation as well as in letters) were vital to Olson's iterations of an archaic "post" modernism, that would, without going backward, create a renewed *polis* and a clearer-sighted citizenry.

I argued in the introduction to the second edition of the correspondence, *The Later Letters*, that Boldereff's effect on twentieth-century poetry and poetics was "incalculably diffusive." She also inspired Olson in his thinking about the breath-line, the typewriter as choreographer, and open-field poetics. A single mother, and a typographical designer, she lived at times in desperate straits as she kept losing jobs in the New York publishing industry owing to what she called her "fiery nature." Her book-design standards were fastidious, and she mourned the carelessness creeping into typography and book design. She was also constantly researching, writing, designing, and self-publishing books on James Joyce's sources (beginning with *Reading Finnegans Wake* in 1959), few of which were reviewed. She had many complaints about the "deadness" of American culture at the time (1950s and early '60s), and she proposed to Olson many theories and texts that supported her own critique and suggested possible remedies. Boldereff did not seem to recognize the post-war renewal of patriarchal authority that underlay these conditions. Olson himself was a remedy, she thought, when she first wrote to him about *Call Me Ishmael* in November 1947. "Every lover of Melville must feel deep gratitude towards you," she wrote, adding that Olson was "one of the ones we so urgently need." She thought, from the beginning of her relationship with Olson, that he would articulate on her behalf a new vision of America. She had many reasons to find American culture too attached to what she called a "depraved sex morality." Undepraved, we might speculate, was her and Olson's love affair. After a few days or nights with Frances, Olson was, in his own opinion, resurrected. She, however, was left alone once again.

Frances's passionate nature, the value of her lively and delightful company, and the immense gift of her letters, including her leads, recommendations, and tips, were never publicly acknowledged by Olson, even when, later on, it may have been safe, so to speak, to do so. Even so, Olson would go into a panic whenever Frances threatened to stop writing to him. He needed her letters, for they kept on setting the path of his thought, and they kept on caring about him and challenging him as a person and as a poet. Ralph, however, characterized Frances as a "Circe" in *Olson at the Harbor*.

There is no doubt that the Olson–Boldereff dynamic is in many ways a nightmare of inequality and double standards. How many times did I roll my eyes or my mind at one of Frances' more florid pronouncements? Must she claim that she and Rimbaud are the same person, not to mention herself and Olson ("I the blood, he the ink")? Must she throw her lot in so completely with male poets and writers, and have absolutely nothing to say about any female writer other than Dora Marsden? (When I asked her about Simone de Beauvoir, she said de Beauvoir was "too much up in her head.") Did she have to use the term "Hebraic" in such a distasteful way? Though she articulated passionately several "programs" for the improvement of the status of women in her time, terms such as "equality" never came up. She advised women to return to what she imagined were the mental and sexual habits of Minoan times. She believed that Nature was to blame for women's debased status — Nature, and women themselves, for reasons she enumerated. She was not in favour of any program to "do away with the sexes"; what she envisioned was the removal of the "thorn" or the "sting" of relations between them. She thought women had become "mentally lazy" and materialistic and unhappy and that all three conditions were related. Yes, she should have been more aware of the ways she rationalized Olson's exploitation of her. Yes, her self-effacement vis-à-vis powerful male writers, her frequent references to "blood" and "race", her admiration of Otto Weininger and other now-suspect theorists of gender such as D.H. Lawrence, could very well compromise the hopes involved in her theories. Boldereff could be described as a masculinist feminist, a truly existential dilemma Rachel Blau du Plessis effectively describes in her chapter on Boldereff in *Purple Passages*.

Because she failed to articulate a sufficiently ideologically rigorous feminism, because she was crafting a vitalist stance on womanhood that was apposite to the problem of the "deadness" of her own times (and images of death and stagnation haunt her condemnations of twentieth century American life), Boldereff has not been taken seriously in intellectual and aesthetic terms. This is not surprising, since Frances was neither an academic nor "a writer," "a writer" being a term she frequently denied applied to her. She was, as she herself admitted, "misled by joy" in her love affair with Olson. And as the engine of Olson's assault on what she first called "the whole inherited puffball," she created a metaphor Olson made his own and which his readers, as well as the subsequent history of American poetics, remain the beneficiary of.

Despite DuPlessis' detailed analysis in *Purple Passages* and a considered appraisal by Ted Byrne in *The Capilano Review*, there has been little acknowledgement of the essential role Boldereff played in the development of projectivist poetics. The critical problem seems to be the distortions of gendered, patriarchal assumptions within projectivist poetics in themselves, if we confine projectivist poetics to Olson's 1950 theory alone and ignore an influence far beyond it, an influence that DuPlessis argued was, for herself, in its opening of form.

Ralph continued to insist that Frances had no significant effect on Olson's writing, even though Olson said she did. After 1950, Olson's chief correspondent was Robert Creeley. Creeley was involved with Black Mountain College; Boldereff was an outsider who thought that Black Mountain College was ruining Olson's life and his writing. She felt his attention shifting far away from her interests and concerns, but for a while was able to reconnect with him via the poetry of Arthur Rimbaud, specifically Rimbaud's poem "Credo in Unam," which Frances translated as "I believe in wholeness."

The current critical trend to delight itself with ahistorical, absolutist enumerations of the errors of the past, including the "patriarchal, racist, white" ideology of Black Mountain College (1933–1957) seems fundamentalist. What is the point? To flatter the infallible ethical standards of the inquisitor? To blame as insufficiently sociologically current Black Mountain College's consciously progressive mandate at that time, in that era in the American South? To deliberately withhold imagination from judgement? What about the catastrophic errors of the present, the ones we are most blind to and most willingly accommodating of? Olson's critique, and his neologism "pejorocracy" are due for renewed methodological attention. As Miriam Nichols writes, Olson's "polemic against Western metaphysics, Plato to Melville, comes of the conviction that humanity has so anthropomorphized its own material life and that of nature that it has mistaken the mental realm of concepts for reality as such."

Everyone involved in the Olson/Boldereff correspondence could be condemned for being less than morally exemplary. Ralph is probably in Purgatory as we speak, regretting his sexist views of Frances. I wish I had done a lot of things differently. Frances once asked Olson to lend her some money but he wouldn't, or couldn't. Frances hurt Olson's feelings with her "more Maximus than you" remark. Olson never publicly acknowledged Frances as a person he loved and cared about. Frances had a destructive effect on both of Olson's marriages. But then, Frances's belief was in "the authority of joy," seemingly no matter what it cost her.

And, she believed in "wholeness." Which is why we need artists, poets, and visionaries; philosophers, mystics, and geniuses; autodidacts, elders, and scholars: for the sake of wholeness. For the sake of the "everything" that is the world and the "everything" that is poetry. For the sake of joy. Sometimes they make fools of themselves. Charles and Frances thought that their mutual project was powerful enough to "dynamite the Patriarchy." What a thought! And, to fortify it, we might imagine being Frances Boldereff that November day in 1947, "standing longingly in front of the Melville shelves" and coming across *Call Me Ishmael* by the relatively unknown Charles Olson who, up to that point, had published only six poems.

BOOK OF MOTZ

Conversations with Frances Boldereff

I met with Frances Motz Boldereff, then Frances Phipps, at her home in Urbana, Illinois while doing research for the editions of her correspondence with Charles Olson I was working on with Ralph Maud. Born in 1906 in Pittsburgh, PA, Frances was a passionate, engaging, talkative woman with whom I had many hours of conversation. During the first of my three visits in the early 1990s I took notes while we were chatting. The selections here are pretty much verbatim.

Money

"Money doesn't really get you anything."

"The New York Public Library has some of the greatest old books in the world. Some wealthy powerful Irish lived and died there and they left the library some marvellous old stuff."

"What the Celts have is a belief that there are powerful things in the world that have nothing to do with politics or money. We don't put our faith in anything. I think we've cheated ourselves. What are we? Who's happy, who's unhappy, and why? Nobody cares."

The Real Theatres of Pittsburgh

"There was this Irish Catholic guy. I begged him to go to bed with me. His father owned all the real theatres in Pittsburgh. Eva Galleon entertained at their elegant house, a limestone mansion. Real black marble floor. The ritzy dog on the front seat beside the chauffeur. The beautiful library upstairs. His little shrinking ascetic mother."

Annie Carol Moore

"One of the greatest children's librarians who ever lived was Annie Carol Moore. She'd been a close friend of Beatrix Potter. She was runnin' the place! She had an old New York accent — she was born there, they pronounced things differently. I was then in my twenties. New York had a library for everybody: Chinese, Polish, Hungarian, Black, and I worked in almost all the branches. The New York Public Library knew how to spend their money, too — every week they sent two bouquets of fresh flowers to every branch, one upstairs in the children's books, one downstairs. I remember a kid, Izzie Witz was his name, he was a poor kid, a lover of beauty and a real reader. He kept coming back week after week for this book of Oscar Wilde's fairy tales, illustrated by du Lac. Of course eventually it disappeared. But I didn't care and Oscar Wilde would have been pleased that he had reached some poor Jewish kid in the Bronx."

Charles Olson

"Charles was nearly dead when I met him darling. He wasn't writing, he had no interest in anything, no pep. We had dinner at the Waldorf all night until closing time. The poor waiter."

*

"His Catholicism was a whole big hunk of life that rated high in his private feelings but that he never talked about."

*

"His was a very heavy demand. I wasn't getting anything back as a woman. 'What the hell does she want? I'm writing to her.'"

*

"His death I read about in the newspaper. I was living in Brooklyn at the time."

*

"When in really deep with Olson in Woodward I designed this book cover — railway tracks diminishing — Motz — Olson —"

*

"I had an image of a slender sailor type, English, thin hips. A voice so marvelous you got a picture of a guy on a ship."

Colbrook

"Very English. In the diplomatic services. You don't even get to take the exams darling unless you're in the upper classes. You read about the English: weirdos! He told me about his really strange mother. No physical contact his whole childhood. She sat in the parlour with a loaded gun on the table beside her. That's the atmosphere under which the poor guy..."

"He had the tremendous good luck of people who don't really want to live."

On "Reading Finnegans Wake"

"My bibliography started off every guy in the business but my name has yet to be mentioned."

On Goya's Etchings

"I first saw 'Los Caprichos' in the rare book room of the New York Public Library. My boyfriend at the time — a member of the diplomatic services — gave me a copy of that book for my birthday."

Sappho

"I had a big thing about her. The first great poetry in Greece was done by a woman."

"I think beauty makes a speech."

Gerry Cooper

"We lived together one summer on the end of Long Island in a cabin with German submarines out in the Sound. One day we went to a resort nearby to swim and lounge around the pool.

Gerry wore a beige Schiaparelli knitted stretch bathing suit that buttoned over one shoulder. In it she looked nude. Me wearing white gloves and carrying a white crocheted purse made Gerry mad. 'Why are you so bourgeois?'"

SCHIAPARELLI

"I had a Schiaparelli skirt — black — off it looked like a rag — but ON! I met Philip Guston wearing this skirt and he never recovered."

BOLDEREFF

"The day before we married he gave away everything darling. His white reindeer jacket, his suede jodhpurs, his silver — threw it all out the window of his apartment in Harlem, for up to that point he had sustained gloriously his bachelorhood through many temptations."

SIMONE DE BEAUVOIR

"Too literary, too prominent, too much the literary woman and not enough out of her own guts."

FEMINISM

"What you are makes the loudest statement."

"When I was in school I lectured the whole high school on being something, not going to the beauty parlour — we discussed income, independence.
 There were loads of women who would never give up being dependent on men. They thought it would give them an easy life, but it doesn't."

NEW YORK CITY
"It was a wonderful place then.
Anyone who went there had the right stuff
(compared to Boston which was Catholic and dull).
It was a nation, it was not one colour.

People didn't take money so seriously.

People are robbed who take money —
the ownership of — as important.

You could be hired on sight, no filling out forms.

I got a job with this Sicilian printer
who was gorgeous and ran the place
like it was Sicily.

One day he had me answer the telephone and
people started coming in just to see who
belonged to that voice."

Boldereff

"Boldereff had been a soldier, a colonel, in the White Russian Army, and head of espionage against the Soviets, and a jurisprudence lawyer. When he came to America, because he was upper-class, they gave him this job as a clerk — a year of apprenticeship during which you make nothing, but just for a year. He said he didn't want it, he turned it down, and painted houses and mowed lawns instead. Anything sensible Boldereff talked himself out of. I met him at a reception. He came in wearing a white reindeer coat. I was twenty-five, he was fifty. He taught me many mentally incorrect attitudes but I was always easily influenced by people. What distinguished a colonel from a private is that a colonel, no matter how drunk or in what condition, when he was needed, when he had to go, he sobered up immediately. So, Motz and Boldereff had spent the night together and Motz rises at 6:30 because she has to get to work. This impressed him so much that it was the turning point — even though we both knew when we first met that we would marry. He came from a wealthy family. The Germans took his house over because it was a very fine house. They took from his wall really beautiful native weavings and cut them up to make horse blankets for their cavalry."

America

"What is the real thing, what are we after? America's lost that, in my opinion."

(I ask when?)

"Fairly early."

(What happened to make it lose it?)

"When the Indians started attacking Americans."

(The Indians?)

"They saw that we don't put our faith in anything."

(Christianity?)

"It's too unimaginative. What is it protecting? Nothing. A bag of bones."

(Will America recover itself?)

"I guess it depends on how goddamn unhappy do we get before we start to wake up."

Notes and Acknowledgements

I am grateful to the many friends, colleagues, event hosts, and editors who have helped this book find its way, among them Michelle Doege, Lindsay Diehl, Heidi Garnett, Richard Osler, Sarah de Leeuw, John Lent, Barry McKinnon, Mona Fertig, James Felton, Penn Kemp, Paul Nelson, Michael Boughn, Tom McGauley, Tom Wayman, Karis Shearer, Julie Bruck, Matt Rader, Erín Moure, Jenny Penberthy, Susan Clark, Pete and Lynn Smith, Duncan McNaughton, Diana Hartog, and the Spoke writing group . I am grateful to the editors of *Canthius, Dispatches* (online); *Arc Poetry Magazine; Dusies, Event,* and especially Sonnet L'Abbe for her generous introduction to "My Education as a Poet" in *The Best Canadian Poetry 2014* anthology. And to Paul Mier, always.

This book is for my brother Murray and my sister Patti.

The references to Dogfish Woman, a personage in Haida mythology, are inspired by an engraved bracelet given to me by my great uncle, who lived in Masset, BC, where my mother grew up in the 1920s and '30s. Her family's social ties with some of the Indigenous families who lived in Old Masset were strong; they revolved around musical evenings, the Anglican Church, and the general store owned by my great-grandfather, James Martin, and the barge *The Bobolink*, piloted by my mother's stepfather Edward Pongs, which delivered supplies and groceries to remote areas. My mother was friends with the Edenshaw girls close to her own age, and later on spent time with other Haida people she knew in Tranquille Sanatarium. The bracelet was signed "XX" and only much later its image was identified, in Queen Charlotte City, as Dogfish Woman and as the work of Victor Adams. Because I had worn this image for decades, Dogfish Woman appears in some poems as a mask for myself and/or my mother. Various depictions of Dogfish Woman are available in "native art" and tourist shops. Dogfish Woman is, among many other thing I don't understand, the power, story, and magic of a species of small shark. Her domed head is sometimes depicted as a tiara or crown. In Bill Reid's iconic canoe, she paddles on the port side.

"The War Against the Imagination": These sentences are excerpted from longer responses to Creative Writing course manuscripts submitted by students for workshopping. "Peak Oil" was written for an open mic event sponsored by Creative Writing students at UBC's Okanagan campus back in about 2010, when the spectre of Peak Oil was in the news.